ALL AMERIC

CW01677576

WW2

WARBIRDS

By F.J. Beerling & M.J. Cleverley

ISBN: 9781919627212

Published by Eagle Star Books Ltd © 2021

Copyright © 2021 Eagle Star Books Ltd

ISBN: 9781919627212

No part of this book shall be reproduced, stored in a retrieval system or Transmitted in any form or by any means, electronic or mechanical, Including photocopying, recording, or by any information retrieval System without prior written permission from the publisher.

F.J. Beerling and M.J. Cleverley assert their rights to be identified As the author and illustrator of this work in accordance with the Copyright, Designs & Patent Act, 1988.

For commissions and enquiries email eaglestarkids@gmail.com

Printed in the UK and the USA

Book design by F.J. Beerling

Although every precaution has been taken in the preparation of this book, The publisher, Author and illustrator assume no responsibility for errors or omissions. Neither is any Liability assumed for damages resulting from the use of this information contained herein.

To my brother Gary and Monique

With love

F.J. Beerling

'Dedicated to all the American aviators who gave their today's for the world's tomorrows'

M.J. Cleverley

Zak sped around the sidewalk corners on his bike as he made his way to school.

Zak was super excited; today was his turn to host the class, end of semester presentation...

...And tomorrow was Veteran's Day, it was November 11th, - Zak's timing was perfect!

Veterans Day

HONORING ALL WHO SERVED

11th November

...Because Zak's presentation was all about American Warbirds and Zak's great grandfather had served in the United States Navy during WW2.

He was a pilot and along with many others, was honored on Veteran's Day.

Zak parked his bike in the bike rack and ran into school.

He high-fived his friends as he made his way down the corridors and into his classroom.

Zak's teacher, Miss Lincoln, had set up the classroom projector and Zak's classmates were already sat at their desks!

"Yikes," said Zak under his breath as he pulled out a memory stick and pushed it into the classroom computer ready to start.

Zak wasn't used to an audience. He was used to getting good grades and studying American military history, which he knew a lot about.

Miss Lincoln, pulled the blinds down and switched the lights off. All eyes were on Zak as he stood at the front of the class and gave his presentation.

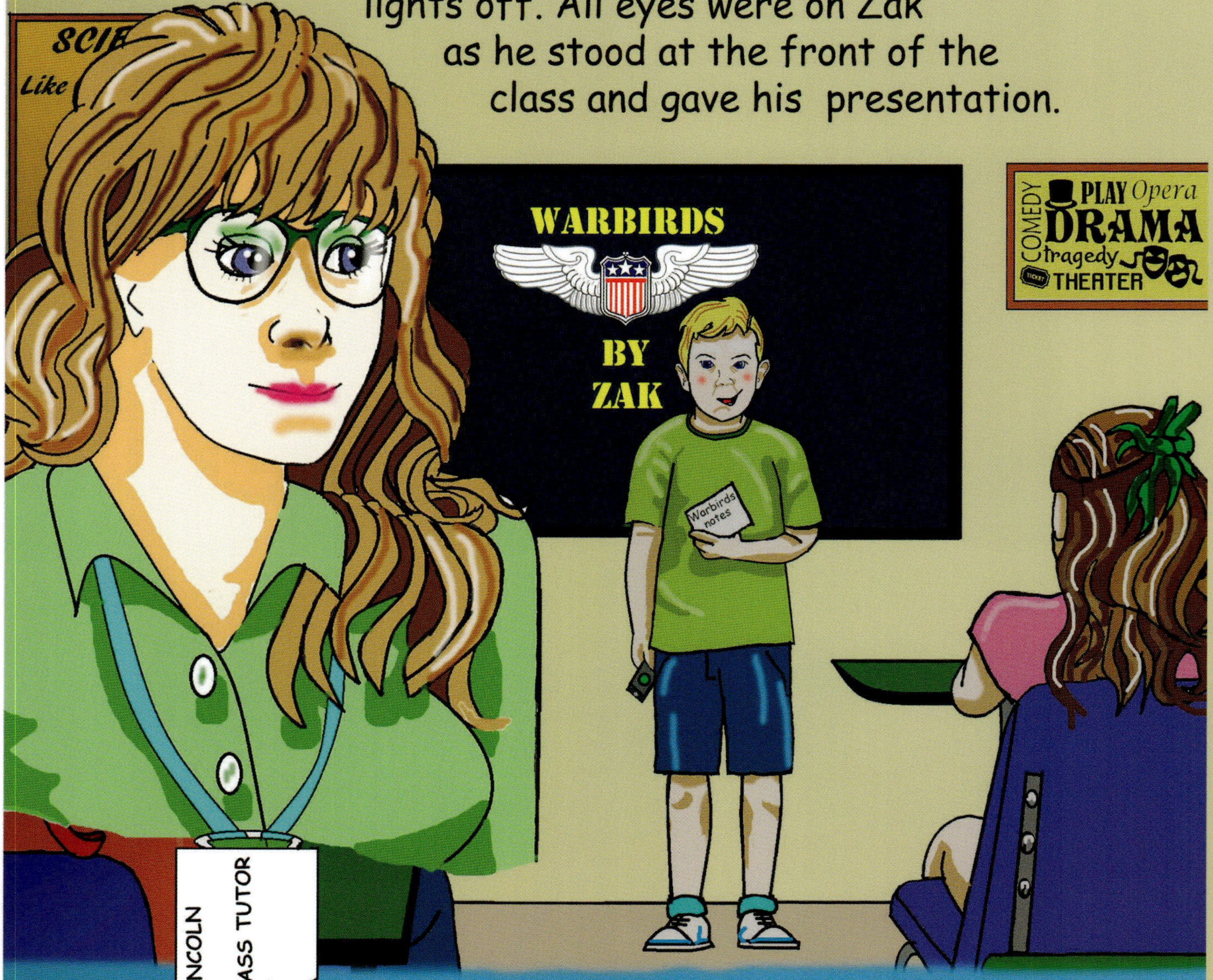

"My great grandfather," Zak said, " served in the United States Navy during WW2. He was a pilot and flew dive bombers!"

Zak's classmates gasped, even Miss Lincoln stopped what she was doing and paid attention to what Zak was saying.

Zak was still nervous when he pressed the remote control and a picture of his great grandfather and a medal appeared on the screen.

"My great grandfather's name was Lieutenant James Johnson. He was a flying ace and in 1943, he was awarded the Distinguished Flying Cross."

Before Zak could continue, Zak's class mates started to clap and cheer...

...The Distinguished Flying Cross, DFC for short was awarded to American Pilots for heroism or extraordinary achievements during aerial combat.

Zak's presentation had started well. Zak wasn't so nervous now; he was keen to talk about all the different types of American aircraft that flew during WW2.

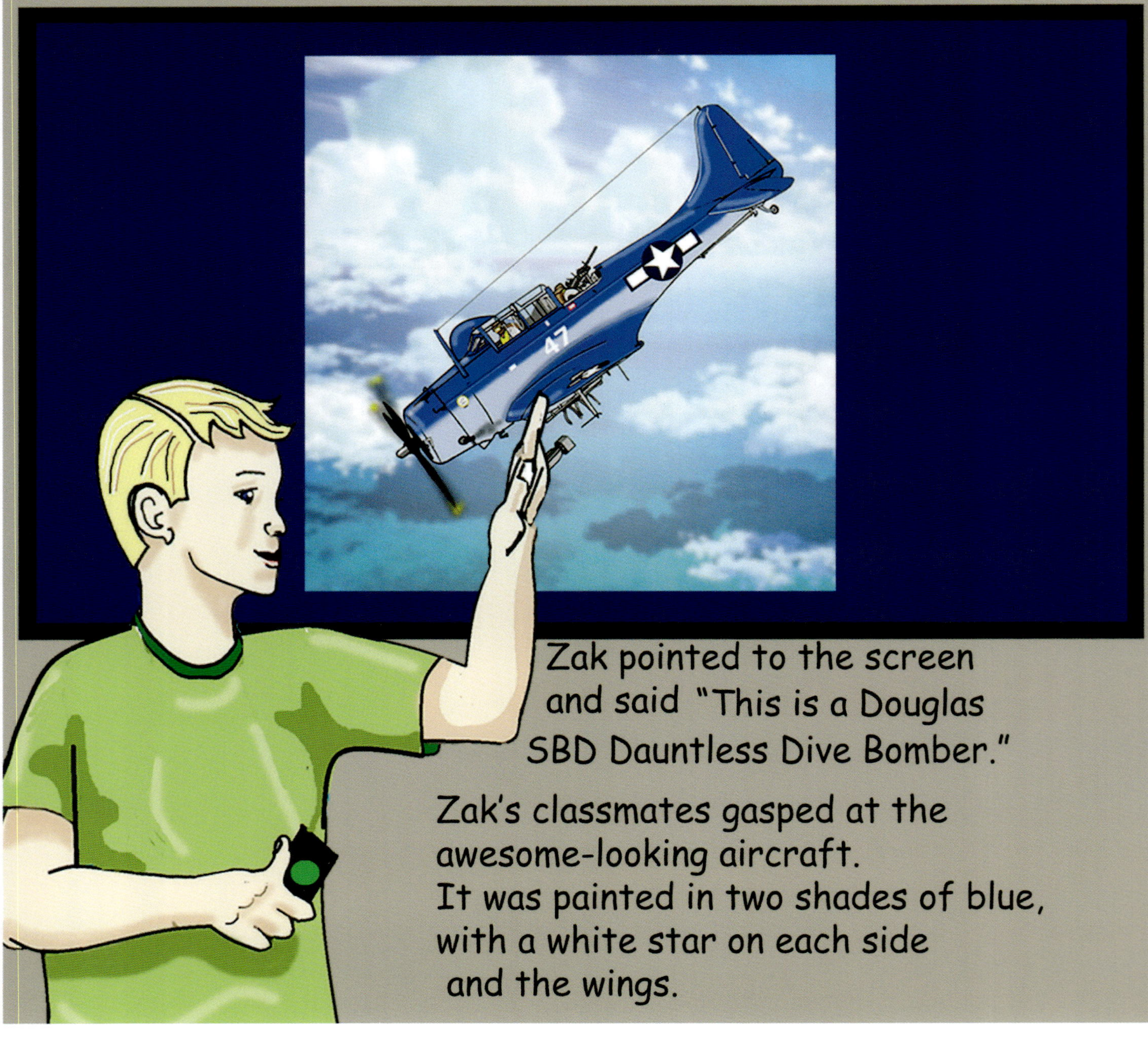

Zak pointed to the screen and said "This is a Douglas SBD Dauntless Dive Bomber."

Zak's classmates gasped at the awesome-looking aircraft.
It was painted in two shades of blue, with a white star on each side and the wings.

Zak continued, "The Douglas SBD was built by the Douglas Aircraft company and the pilots that flew it during the war nicknamed it 'Slow But Deadly,' or SBD for short. The SBD really stood for 'Scout Bomber Douglas'...

...Which my great grandfather flew during the war.

Dive bomber pilots aimed their bombs by bravely diving right down onto the target while it was trying to shoot them out of the sky!"

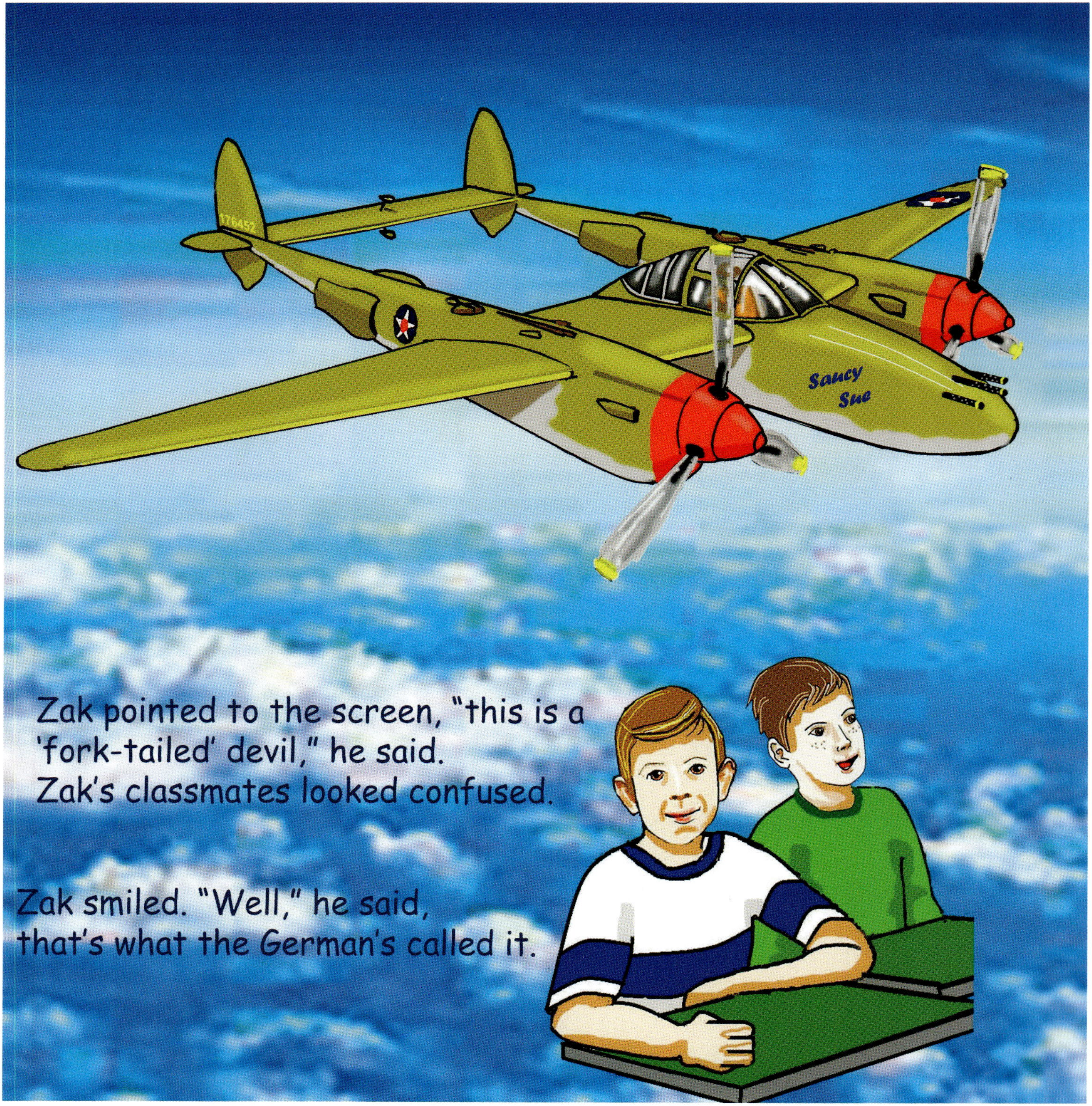

Zak pointed to the screen, "this is a 'fork-tailed' devil," he said.
Zak's classmates looked confused.

Zak smiled. "Well," he said, that's what the German's called it.

It was really called a Lockheed P-38 Lightning – a fast, two tailed plane that had just one seat for the pilot...
...It was a very effective fighter plane, and operated at night! It could also drop bombs.

Zak's nerves had almost gone and his classmates were learning a lot about the different types of American aircraft that were used during WW2.

Zak pushed the button and a Curtis P-40 Warhawk appeared on the screen.

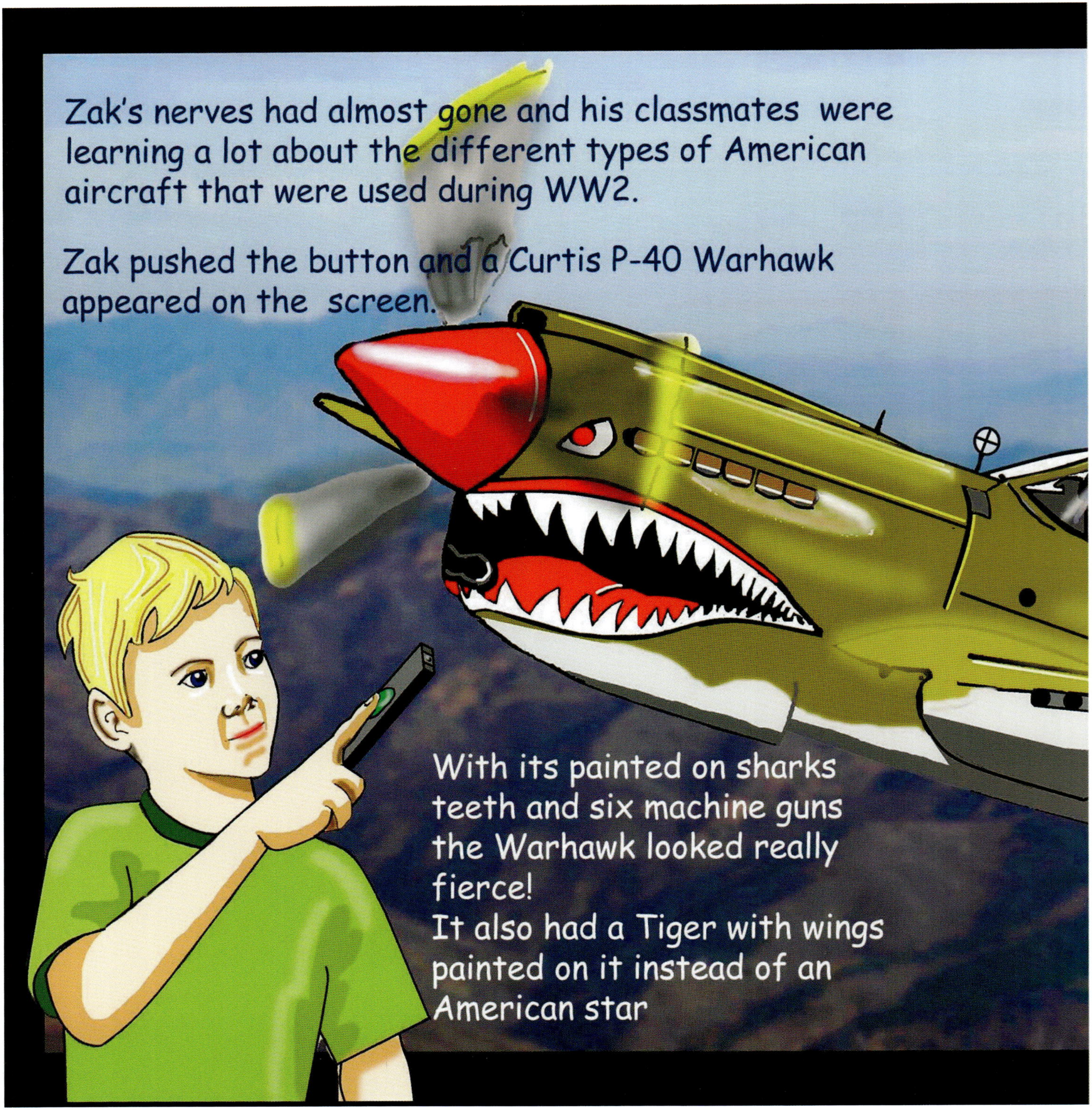

With its painted on sharks teeth and six machine guns the Warhawk looked really fierce!
It also had a Tiger with wings painted on it instead of an American star

This was because before America entered WW2 some volunteer American pilots famously known as 'The Flying Tigers' flew them on secret missions as they tried to defend China against a Japanese invasion.

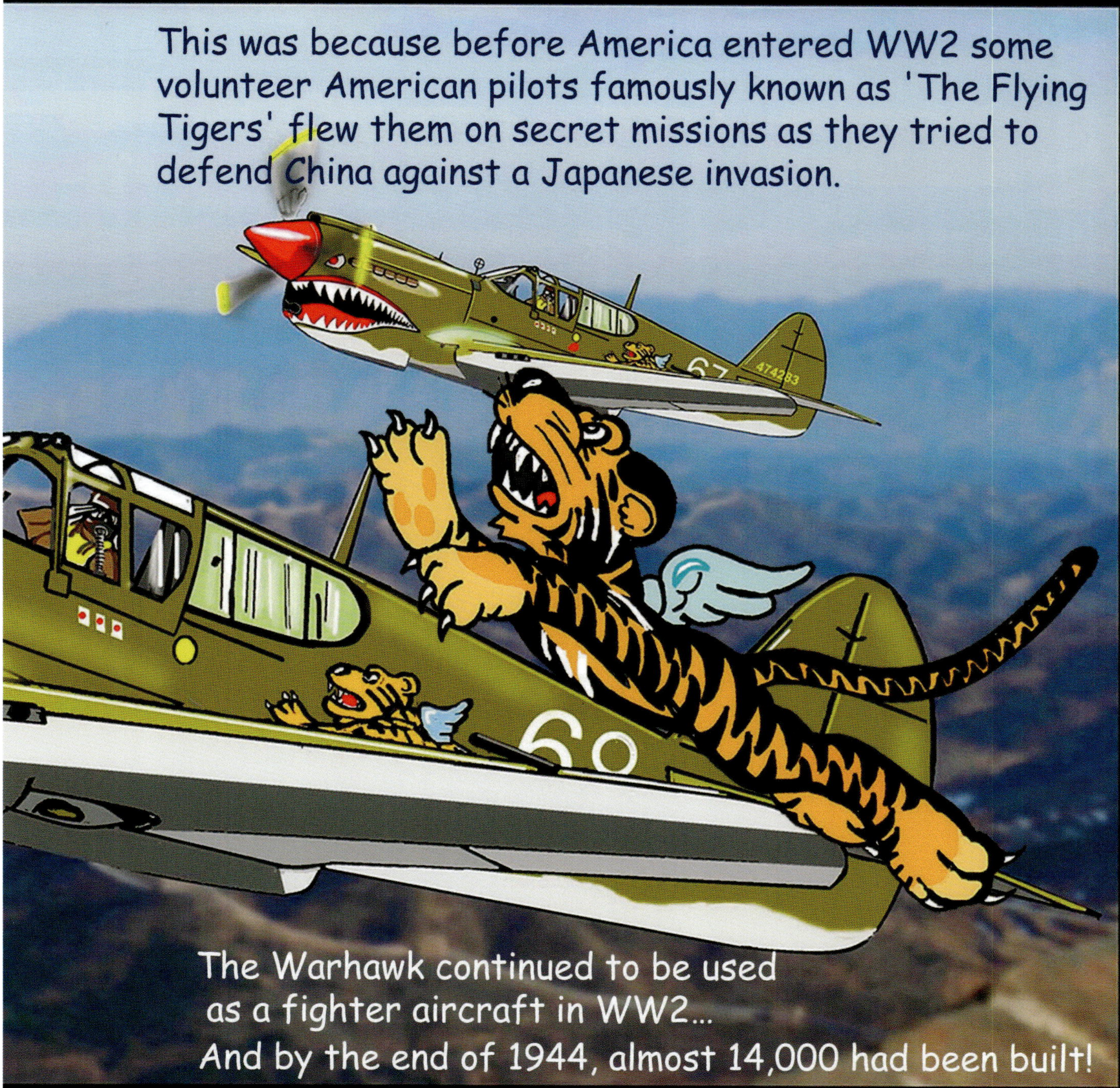

The Warhawk continued to be used as a fighter aircraft in WW2...
And by the end of 1944, almost 14,000 had been built!

Zak's classmates were taking notes and Miss Lincoln was taking down old paintings to make room for Zak's all - American WW2 aircraft, which the pupils would paint after Zak's presentation.
BOMBS AWAY!
Zak continued. He pressed a button and a big Consolidated B-24 Liberator plane appeared on the screen.
"This is a Flying Boxcar," said Zak.

Well, as soon as he said that his classmates began to laugh. What a silly name for an aircraft!

Zak explained. "It was called the 'Flying Boxcar,' because it looked like a railroad boxcar carriage...square!"

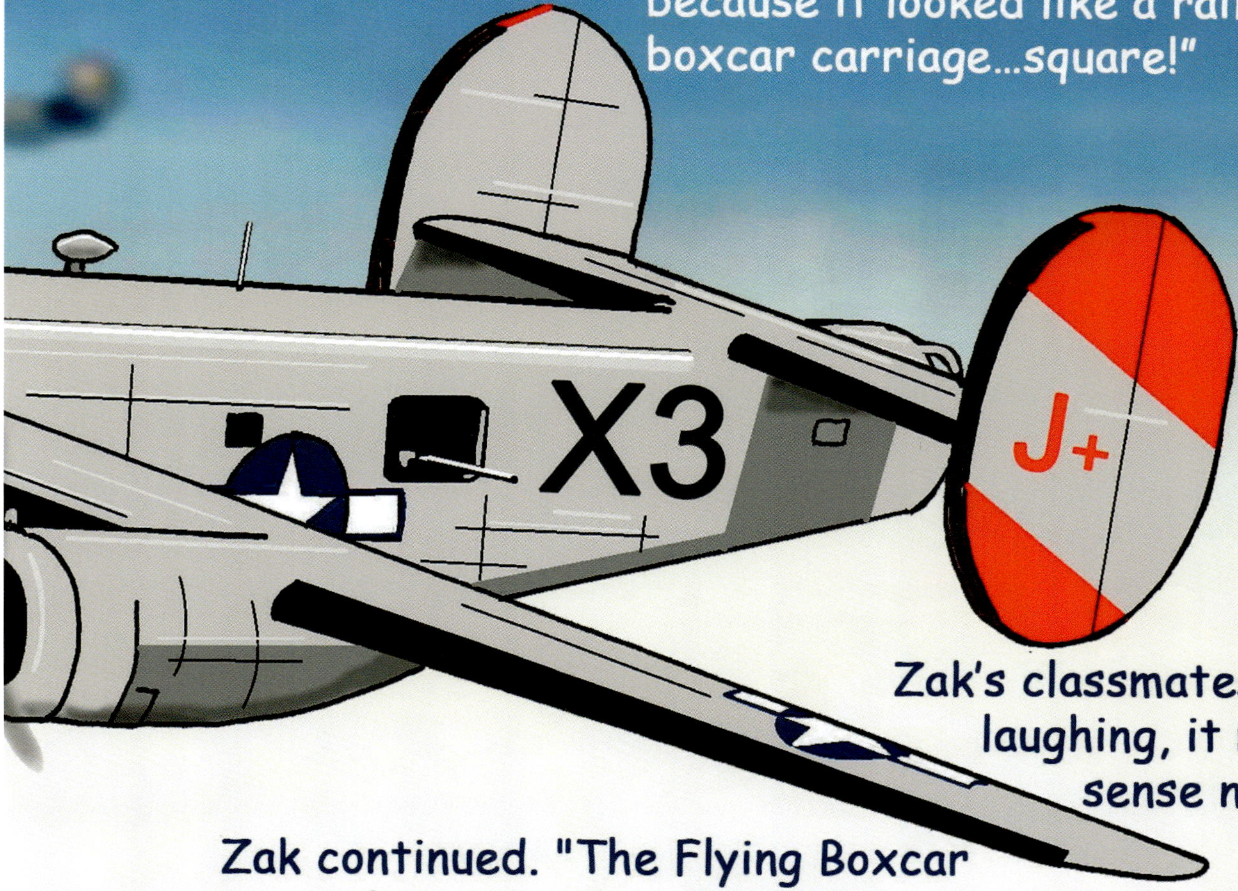

Zak's classmates stopped laughing, it made sense now.

Zak continued. "The Flying Boxcar was a heavy bomber. Its unique wing design gave it the ability to fly very high up. It also had a a long range and could carry a heavy bomb load...

...it was also the first bomber to fly across the Atlantic ocean to Britain and back on a regular basis.

The next plane to appear on screen was the Grumman F6F Hellcat. It was a newly designed fighter when it first went into combat in September of 1943.

"The Hellcat," said Zak, "was an aircraft carrier-based fighter plane. This meant it had to be able to take off and land from short distances – ideal for a bucking aircraft carrier deck in rough seas."

Zak continued. "In just two years 12,275 Hellcat's were built! They did well in dogfights above the Pacific ocean." Zak's classmates looked puzzled again, so Zak came to their rescue.
"Dogfights," said Zak "are 'one on one' battles with enemy planes in the sky."
21
21
Zak's classmates got it now.

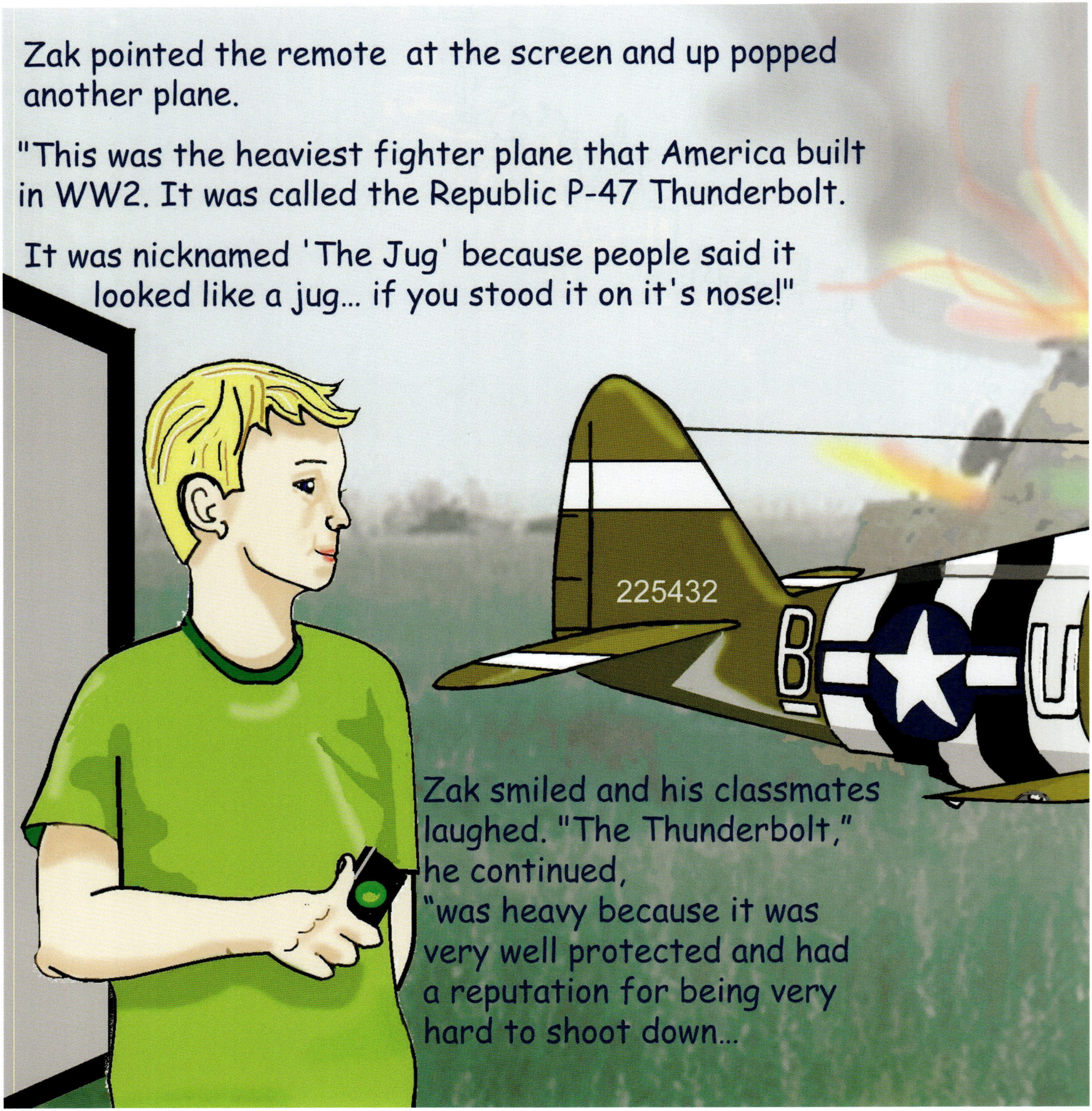
Zak pointed the remote at the screen and up popped another plane.
"This was the heaviest fighter plane that America built in WW2. It was called the Republic P-47 Thunderbolt.
It was nicknamed 'The Jug' because people said it looked like a jug... if you stood it on it's nose!"
225432
Zak smiled and his classmates laughed. "The Thunderbolt," he continued, "was heavy because it was very well protected and had a reputation for being very hard to shoot down...

...It was heavily armed with guns and was ideal for dogfights at high altitude.

It was also brilliant at attacking targets that were on the ground.

It could even be armed with rockets which made it able to destroy armored targets such as tanks – it became known as a 'Tank buster'!"

"And now," said Zak, "onto my all-time favourite American Aircraft, the world-famous Boeing B-17 bomber also known as the, 'Flying Fortress."

Uh-oh, Zak's classmates had that puzzled look on their faces again,
So once again Zak explained.

"It was called the Flying Fortress because it had heavy firepower in gun emplacements - almost like a fort up in the air...

...Like a lot of American planes the crews painted pictures on them and gave them names. The mostfamous B-17 was called Memphis Belle."

Zak's classmates had all heard of the Memphis Belle.

After all it had inspired two movies - one was a documentary and the other a Hollywood Blockbuster called, Memphis Belle.

It was the first B-17 heavy bomber to complete 25 combat missions over Germany!
A few B-17's are on display in museums all around the world. And some are even today in a flightworthy condition!

The B-17 Flying Fortress had caused quite a stir among Zak's classmates.

They wanted Miss Lincoln to take them on a field trip to an aviation museum so they could see them on display.

It was almost time for recess so Zak rushed through the rest of his presentation. He pushed the button and a Douglas C-47 Skytrain appeared on the screen.

.....different countries knew it by different names...
....we Americans nicknamed it the 'Gooney Bird' because it looked a bit like the big goofy and clumsy bird in the Pacific islands." continued Zak.
"Hundreds of these aircraft were used to drop allied paratroopers on enemy targets during DDay in France in June 1944."
2X
Whistling Dixie
COMEDY
tragedy
TICKET
Zak paused now and looked around at his classmates. They were in awe and learning so much about these amazing aircraft. Zak was pleased with how his presentation was going.

Miss Lincoln was so proud of Zak.

Zak was shy, he had never given a presentation before. He had never stood in front of the class before.

"This was the P-51 'Mustang' named after the wild horse with a powerful kick if you're fool enough to get in its way...

...The P-51 was a long-range single-seat fighter," said Zak.

Zak's classmates were fascinated, Zak continued.
" It's powerful engine was the same as in the famous British fighter The 'Spitfire'.
Rebel Yell
From late 1943, P-51's became the first fighters that could protect our bombers in raids all the way from England to Germany...
...Even after WW2, the P51 was later used in the Korean War and other conflicts."

Zak, with his new found confidence pointed the remote one last time and a massive silver aircraft appeared on the screen.

It was a Boeing B-29 Super Fortress.

Zak's classmates looked puzzled once more. Zak smiled and said, "Like the B-17 Flying Fortress, it was designed for high-altitude bombing.

It became the only aircraft to ever use nuclear weapons during combat. It was this Superfortress named 'enola Gay' after the pilot's mom, that dropped the first of the two atom bombs on Japan which then ended WW2."

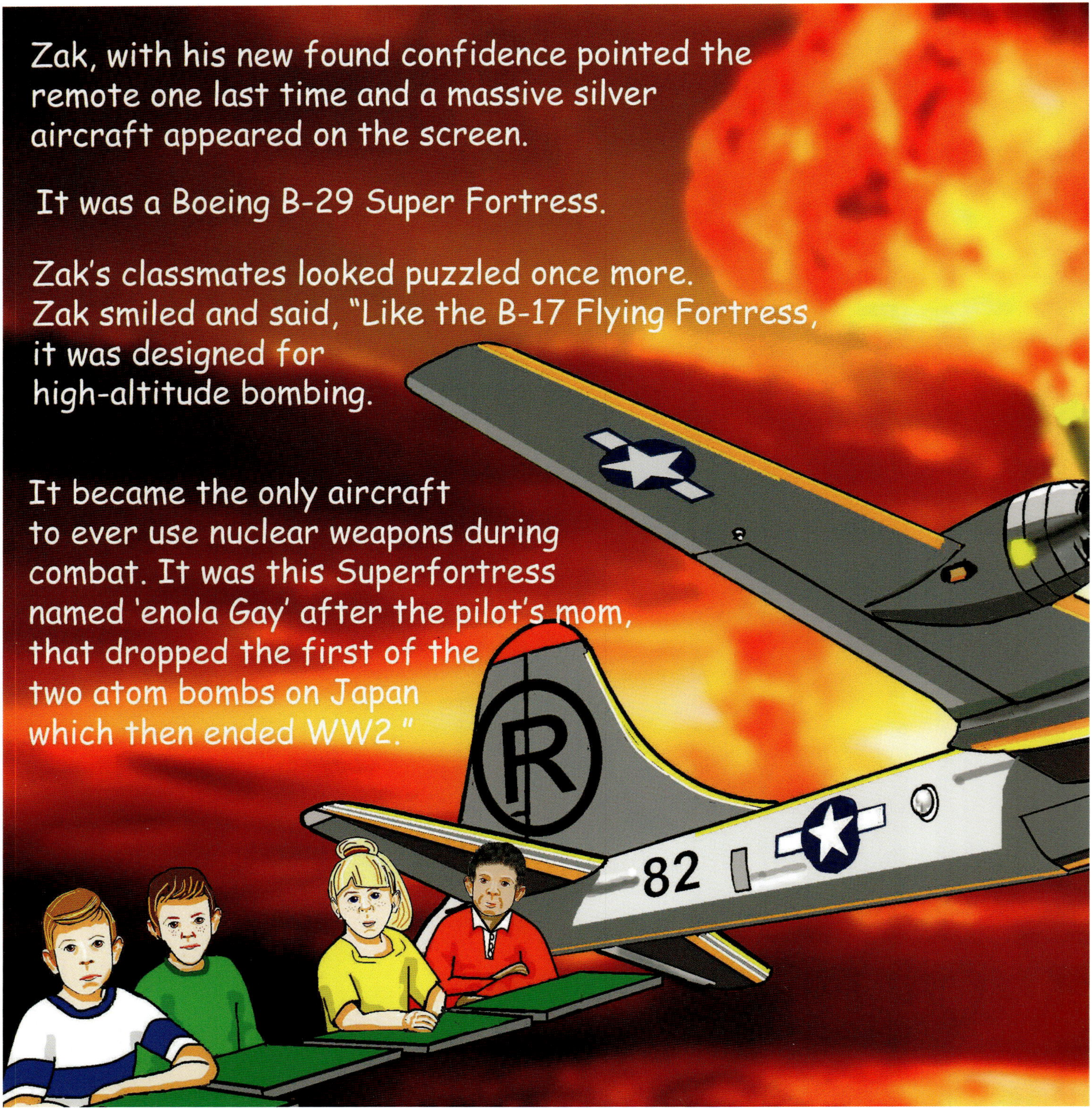

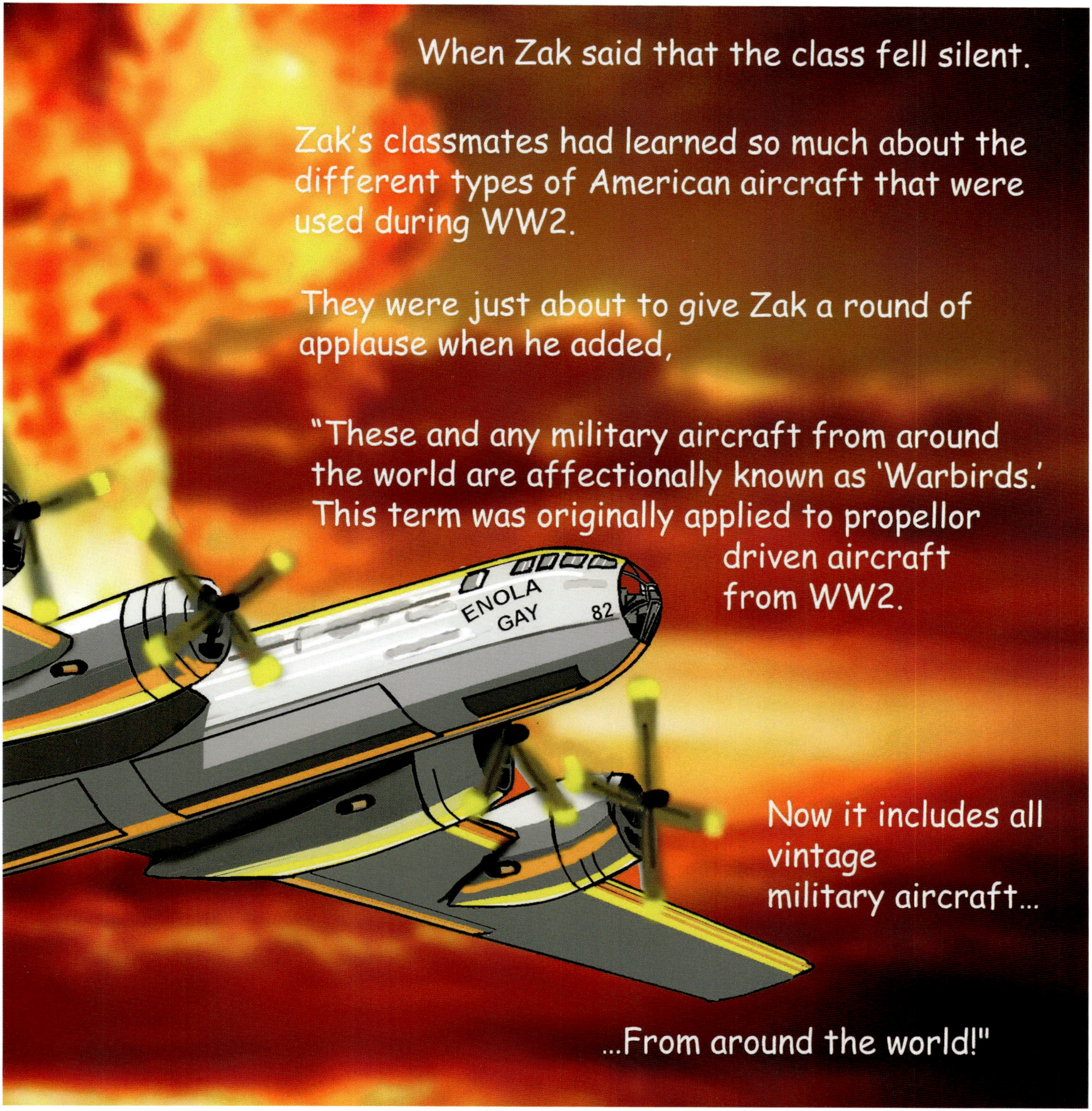

When Zak said that the class fell silent.

Zak's classmates had learned so much about the different types of American aircraft that were used during WW2.

They were just about to give Zak a round of applause when he added,

"These and any military aircraft from around the world are affectionally known as 'Warbirds.' This term was originally applied to propellor driven aircraft from WW2.

Now it includes all vintage military aircraft...

...From around the world!"

Zak's presention was over.

Mrs Lincoln and Zak's classmates gave Zak a big round of applause. Zak had the biggest smile on his face; his presentation was a success.

Zak was a star!

Many of his classmates had been inspired by Zak that day.

It's not easy to stand up and give a talk to a class full of pupils and keep them interested.

The very next day Miss Lincolm took Zak and all his classmates to their local air museum....

...as it was Veteran's Day, they were invited to sit with retired veteran's and were treated to some lunch.

They waved their flags and listened to the veteran's as they shared their stories...

...It was an amazing day out and at the end of it they all sang 'The Star-Spangled Banner', before having their photos taken with the Veterans and museum workers.

What an amazing way to celebrate Veteran's Day.

God Bless America!

139401
51 C
A26 INVADER